BECOMING ONE

Weekly Insights
to Nurture Your Marriage

Kerry Pappas
Center for Family Care
Greek Orthodox Archdiocese of America

HOLY CROSS
ORTHODOX PRESS

Brookline, Massachusetts

©2024 Greek Orthodox Archdiocese of America
Published by
Holy Cross Orthodox Press
Hellenic College, Inc.
50 Goddard Avenue
Brookline, MA 02445

On the cover: Icon of Saints Joachim and Anna by Erin Kimmet

ISBN: 978-1-935317-05-0

Publisher's Cataloging in Publication
(Provided by Cassidy Cataloging Services, Inc.)
Names: Pappas, Kerry, author. | Greek Orthodox Archdiocese of
    America. Center for Family Care, sponsoring body.
Title: Becoming one : insights to nurture your marriage / Kerry
    Pappas ; Center for Family Care, Greek Orthodox Archdiocese
    of America.
Description: Brookline, Massachusetts : Holy Cross Orthodox
    Press, [2024] | Includes bibliographical references.
Identifiers: ISBN: 978-1-935317-05-0
Subjects: LCSH: Marriage--Religious aspects--Orthodox Eastern
    Church. | Love--Religious aspects-- Orthodox Eastern Church.
    | Forgiveness--Religious aspects--Orthodox Eastern Church. |
    Emotional intelligence--Religious aspects--Orthodox Eastern
    Church. | Commitment (Psychology)--Religious aspects--Orthodox Eastern Church. | Orthodox Eastern Church-- Doctrines. | LCGFT: Devotional literature.
Classification: LCC: BX378.M2 P36 2024 | DDC:
    261.8/35810882819--dc23

To Harry,

by the grace of God,

my beloved husband of 43 years

v

INTRODUCTION

"Teacher, which is the great commandment in the law?

'You shall love the Lord your God with all your heart, and with all your soul, and with all your mind.' This is the greatest and first commandment. And a second is like it: 'You shall love your neighbor as yourself.'" (Matt. 22:37–39)

As Christ taught in response to the question posed by a Pharisee, the greatest commandment is to love God, and the second is to love our neighbor. As married people, our closest daily neighbor is our spouse, the person to whom we have been joined by Christ as "one flesh" in the sacrament of marriage.

In the wedding service, the priest leads the community in many prayers and petitions on behalf of the couple, including that Christ will join them as "one flesh" and grant them "concord of soul and body," and "oneness of mind."

Christ acts decisively in the sacrament of marriage, abundantly blessing the couple, not only when they come to the church to be married, but throughout their lives.

Thus, the sacrament is the beginning of the life-long journey of the couple to continuously invoke the grace of God in their marriage in order to become sanctified and to more fully realize oneness. Similar to salvation—we are saved by what Christ has done for us through the Cross and Resurrection and by virtue of our baptism; yet, we are constantly in a state of being saved. The question then becomes for each couple: Will we go about marriage intentionally seeking to grow toward the full realization of oneness that Christ bestowed on us on our wedding day, and thus come to realize the sacramental union, or will we simply remember the wedding service fondly and go about life with little regard for growing what He has given us?

In the midst of the numerous responsibilities of daily life, husband and wife can lose sight of one another and begin to take God's grace and one another for granted. "Oneness" is not an automatic; it requires a continual invocation of God's grace and presence, coupled with hard work on our part. Thus, the title of this small book, *Becoming One*. Christ joins us as "one flesh" in the sacrament; however, growing toward oneness of mind and heart, concord of soul and body, is a continual process of growth.

The purpose of this small workbook is to offer couples a simple and doable 52-week (one year) framework for nurturing marriage and growing oneness and connection. Each entry is self-contained and offers a principle or theme applicable to marriage, though as you will see, some themes have more than one entry. The entries come from a wide variety of resources.

In order to most effectively utilize this resource, couples are encouraged to:

- Create a consistent weekly sacred space of 20–30 minutes.
- Begin with two minutes of silence and then pray the Lord's Prayer together.
- Read, prayerfully consider, and discuss the brief quotation for the week and the question(s) that follow. Some weeks will include a specific task to work on; others will not.
- Use the space for notes to jot down what you want to remember from the discussion.
- Practice and incorporate the theme of the week's quotation each day of the upcoming week.

- When you meet the next week, take the first few minutes to discuss the impact of incorporating the prior week's principle into your marriage.

If, as you attend to your marriage in specific ways each week, you happen to encounter a bump, something creating increased tension in your marriage, it may be a signal that you may need some support to work through a particular issue or dynamic in your marriage. In such a circumstance, please reach out to your parish priest or a counselor.

May the Lord bless you and draw you nearer to oneness of mind and heart as you set aside a specific time and space to intentionally focus on one another and your marriage with a commitment to incorporating what you have read and discussed in the upcoming week.

Finally, and most importantly, as you work through these entries, remember that God is the Source and Provider of love. He desires for us to have healthy, wholesome, marriages full of His love, mercy, joy, and compassion. In engaging each entry, begin with prayer, asking the Lord to love your spouse through you and trusting His Word that "where two or three are gathered together in my name, I am there among them" (Matt. 18:20).

CONTENTS

Week 1
MY CLOSEST NEIGHBOR 2

Week 2
CRITICAL OR VULNERABLE? .4

Week 3
HABITS OF LOVE 6

Week 4
MARRIAGE STABILITY 8

Week 5
THE OLDEST TRICK IN THE BOOK 10

Week 6
THE MANY FACES OF LOVE .12

Week 7
PATIENCE 14

Week 8
KINDNESS 16

Week 9
LOVE IS NOT 18

Week 10
LEADERSHIP *AND* HUMBLE SERVITUDE 20

Week 11
FORGIVENESS (Part 1) 22

Week 12
FORGIVENESS (Part 2) 24

Week 13
FRIENDSHIP 26

Week 14
AN IMPORTANT PRIORITY 28

Week 15
MARRIAGE IS A "BOAT" 30

Week 16
WHY WORRY? 32

Week 17
THE MYSTERY OF MARRIAGE 34

Week 18
"FILL THEIR HOUSES . . ." 36

Week 19
TWO ARE BETTER THAN ONE 38

Week 20
STRETCHED TO THE LIMIT? 40

Week 21
A KEY TO NAVIGATING CONFLICT? 42

Week 22
MARRIAGE IS A JOURNEY OF EXPLORATION 44

Week 23
LIVING WITH AMBIGUITY 46

Week 24
APPRECIATION 49

Week 25
RUPTURE AND REPAIR 50

Week 26
A PLACE FOR SILENCE (Part 1) 52

Week 27
A PLACE FOR SILENCE (Part 2) 54

Week 28
HARMONY (Part 1) 56

Week 29
HARMONY (Part 2) 58

Week 30
MEANINGFUL CONVERSATION 60

Week 31
EVERYDAY A FEAST DAY 62

Week 32
MARRIAGE IS MORE THAN HUMAN 64

Week 33
PLEASANT WORDS 66

Week 34
RIGHT OR WRONG? 68

Week 35
DISCIPLINE AND SELF-DENIAL 70

Week 36
CULTIVATING LOVE 72

Week 37
LOVE AND HARMONY 74

Week 38
THE DIVINE IN THE ORDINARY 76

Week 39
REPENT...................................78

Week 40
PERFECTION? 80

Week 41
CONFRONTING SIN AND WEAKNESS 82

Week 42
EMOTIONAL INTELLIGENCE 84

Week 43
DRAWING NEAR TO GOD 86

Week 44
WORDS OF CONSOLATION 88

Week 45
FINANCE 90

Week 46
LISTENING AS HOSPITALITY .92

Week 47
COMMITMENT AND TRUST .94

Week 48
THE OVERARCHING LITMUS TEST 96

Week 49
RITUALS 98

Week 50
THE EXPERIENCE OF LOVE 100

Week 51
WHAT DO WE SEE? 102

Week 52
WISDOM FOR CONFLICT 104

Bonus 1
OBEDIENCE 106

Bonus 2
"THE" RULE OF MARRIAGE 108

Bonus 3
LISTENING 110

Bonus 4
FIDELITY 112

Bonus 5
UNITY 114

Bonus 6
EMOTIONAL CAPITAL 116

Acknowledgments 119

Quotation Sources 119

BECOMING ONE

Week 1

MY CLOSEST NEIGHBOR

Quotation

"You shall love the Lord your God with all your heart, and with all your soul, and with all your mind. This is the great and first commandment. And a second is like it, You shall love your neighbor as yourself." (Matt. 22:37–39)

Reflection

For those who are married, these words of Jesus are a daily reminder of the most important priorities in life; first, to love God, and secondly, to love our neighbor as ourselves. And who is your closest neighbor? Your spouse!

For Discussion

1. Consider your spouse as your closest "neighbor" and discuss the possible ramifications for your marriage.
2. How do you and your spouse support one another to grow in love for God?
3. What do you do well in loving one another as closest neighbors?
4. How can you do better? Be specific and decide together on one step you will take to better love your spouse as yourself.

Week 2

CRITICAL OR VULNERABLE?

Quotation

"Friendship and love are impossible without a mutual vulnerability." (Henri Nouwen*)

Reflection

Too often in marriage we criticize our spouse, masking a hurt we feel in an angry comment. Saying something like, "You're always checking your phone!" (critical) may, in fact, be a way of communicating, "I want more of your attention" (vulnerable). Or, "You never come to church with the family" communicates "I really want you to come to church."

For Discussion

1. What is one area of vulnerability you tend to mask with criticism in relating to your spouse?

2. In the coming week, prayerfully work on replacing criticism with vulnerability, and thus becoming more truthful with your spouse. At the end of the week, discuss the impact of the increased vulnerability and decreased criticism.

---

*Dutch Catholic priest, professor, writer, and theologian.

Week 3

HABITS OF LOVE

Quotation

"Love . . . is not merely a feeling. It is a deep
unity, maintained by the will and deliberately
strengthened by habit: reinforced by . . . the grace
which both partners ask, and receive, from God."
(C. S. Lewis)

Reflection

Read carefully these words of C.S. Lewis and consider love as a feeling but more importantly as a deep unity, which requires God's grace and effort on the part of the couple.

For Discussion

1. What deliberate habits do you practice to both maintain and grow the unity in your marriage?
2. How do you invoke the grace of God for your marriage?
3. Brainstorm together and decide on one new specific habit you will form as a couple to grow your marriage unity. Make sure the habit is manageable and doable.
4. Pray together for God's grace to be vigilant in maintaining the new habit.

Week 4

MARRIAGE STABILITY

Quotation

". . . you must have at least five times as many positive as negative moments together if your marriage is to be stable." (John Gottman*)

Reflection

Five to one is the general rule of thumb specialists in the field of relationships teach regarding positive to negative statements, and here, we learn that the same applies to moments together.

For Discussion

1. Recall and share with one another five recent positive moments.

2. Recall and share with one another one recent negative moment.

3. Commit to writing one positive moment on a notecard each day for the coming week and putting it into a jar. At the end of the week, read what you have written out loud to one another and discuss the impact of recalling the positives.

*American psychologist and author, specializing in marriage research and therapy.

THE OLDEST TRICK IN THE BOOK

Quotation

"The man said, 'The woman whom you gave to be with me, she gave me fruit from the tree, and I ate.' Then the Lord God said to the woman, 'What is this that you have done?' The woman said, 'The serpent tricked me, and I ate.'" (Gen. 3:12–13)

Reflection

The story of the fall of humanity provides us with an important lesson for marriage—taking responsibility. When conflict arises, we may respond with a knee-jerk reaction of placing blame on our spouse and pointing the finger at him/her, rather than looking first at ourselves and our role in the conflict.

For Discussion

1. What is your tendency when conflict arises? To point the finger or take appropriate responsibility for your part in the conflict?

2. In the next week, whenever you and your spouse disagree, pause and consider your part in the disagreement before you speak. Then, after several days, discuss the impact of this "pause" on your marriage.

THE MANY FACES OF LOVE

Quotation

"Love is patient, love is kind. It does not envy, it does not boast, it is not proud. It does not dishonor others, it is not self-seeking, it is not easily angered, it keeps no record of wrongs. Love does not delight in evil but rejoices with the truth. It always protects, always trusts, always hopes, always perseveres."
(1 Cor. 13:4–7)

Reflection

Sit with your spouse and silently read this passage. Then take turns reading it aloud to each other, replacing "love" with your name.

For Discussion

1. Share with your spouse how he/she manifests most strikingly the love of Christ in your marriage.
2. Share with your spouse the one face of love that is most difficult for you to practice.
3. Consider what you can do to grow in this one area.

Week 7

PATIENCE

Quotation

"Love is Patient . . ." (1 Cor. 13:4)

Reflection

The Greek word for patience in this passage is the same word used in the response following each Gospel reading on Holy Thursday night, "Glory to your *long-suffering*, Lord, glory to you."

For Discussion

1. Prayerfully reflect with your spouse on how long-suffering is manifested in your love for one another. It may involve—enduring an annoying habit; navigating marriage with one spouse suffering from a chronic physical, emotional, or mental condition; a recurring point of contention . . .

2. Consider and discuss how to support one another as you seek to grow in patience in your marriage relationship as you "bear with one another." (Col. 3:13)

Week 8

KINDNESS

Quotation

"Love is kind . . ." (1 Cor. 13:4)

Reflection

Take a few moments and sit quietly beside one another, reflecting on what kindness means and looks like to you.

For Discussion

1. Share with one another your understanding of kindness, particularly in the context of marriage.

2. Considering the New Testament meaning of kindness as "useful" or "well-suited" (akin to acts of kindness), how do you show kindness to your spouse?

3. Share with your spouse a recent kindness he/she extended to you in either word or deed.

4. Prayerfully consider and enact one additional small "kindness" you will offer your spouse each day.

Week 9

LOVE IS NOT...

Quotation

"Love is not boastful or arrogant or rude . . ." (1 Cor. 13:4b–5a)

Reflection

In other words, "love does not brag, show off or need attention; it is not puffed or blown up like bellows; and it does not act unbecomingly, improperly or indecently."

For Discussion

1. Consider and share with your spouse any ways in which you see yourself as being boastful, arrogant or rude toward him/her.

2. Give your spouse an opportunity to *lovingly* share with you anything you may have missed.

3. Then, ask forgiveness of one another and "repent." That is, make a firm commitment, invoking the grace of God, to not engage in such behaviors.

Week 10

LEADERSHIP *AND* HUMBLE SERVITUDE

Quotation

"The wife is the noble lady of the household, but also the mature servant. The husband is the captain of the household but also the lowest laborer." (St. Paisios)

Reflection

Much has been written about the role of husband and wife. Using imagery, St. Paisios offers a fresh and wise perspective, one that accounts for the shared servant leadership both husband and wife are called to in marriage. One of the blessed opportunities all married couples encounter is to learn how to "share" both leadership and servanthood.

For Discussion

1. Discuss the areas in which each of you takes leadership in your marriage.
2. Discuss the areas in which each of you is more of the "mature servant" or "lowest laborer."
3. In which areas do you both exercise both leadership and servanthood?

FORGIVENESS
(Part 1)

Quotation

"Genuine forgiveness is one of the most intimate acts of marriage because it draws husband and wife into the depths of divine grace and into the heart of the other." (Anonymous)

Reflection

The practice of forgiveness is necessary for a growing and thriving marriage. Consider and discuss what that practice presently looks like in your marriage. Is it an exceptional occurrence with "big" offenses, an occasional "I'm sorry" met with a shrug, a daily perfunctory exchange to cover "everything" in each day, or a consistent, sincere, and authentic mutual exchange?

For Discussion

1. Remembering that the source of all forgiveness is Christ, discuss with your spouse specific incidences in which you have extended forgiveness to one another and how in doing so, experienced both the grace of God and a window into the heart of your spouse.

2. What works well for you in your practice of forgiveness?

3. How can you better seek and extend forgiveness to one another?

Week 12

FORGIVENESS
(Part 2)

Quotation

"The sign of sincere love is to forgive wrongs done to us. It was with such love that the Lord loved the world." (St. Mark the Ascetic)

Reflection

When two people live in the intimate relationship of marriage, it is inevitable that both "wrong" one another. If we are honest with ourselves and our spouse, these wrongs occur more often than we like to think. We may ignore and become insensitive to the "small" wrongs and only pay attention to the "bigger" wrongs. Practicing together a discipline of naming daily wrongs and then exchanging forgiveness cultivates "sincere love," that is, the love of God in Jesus Christ.

For Discussion

1. Thus far today, name the ways in which you have wronged or sinned against your spouse. Remember to consider both sins of commission and sins of omission, that is what you have done (e.g., used unkind words) and what you have failed to do (e.g., not shown physical affection knowing that your spouse primarily receives love through touch).

2. Determine together a "practice" of forgiveness you want to follow.

3. For the next week, take time each evening to name the ways in which you have sinned against your spouse on that day, then exchange mutual forgiveness.

Week 13

FRIENDSHIP

Quotation

"One of the simple secrets to lasting love is feeding the flames of friendship . . . the underpinning of friendship and positive regard . . . makes a relationship truly great." (John Gottman* and Nan Silver**)

Reflection

A newly engaged bride-to-be expressed with exuberance, "I am going to marry my best friend!" A deep, abiding, and growing friendship is foundational to a stable and healthy marriage. However, husband and wife may get so consumed by the responsibilities of daily life that they fail to feed the friendship.

For Discussion

1. What do you do to "feed the flames of friendship" with your spouse?
2. Determine together one new practice you will put into place to nurture your friendship.

---

* American psychologist and author, specializing in marriage research and therapy.
** Author, journalist, and editor.

Week 14

AN IMPORTANT PRIORITY

Quotation

"Seek first to understand, then to be understood."
(St. Francis of Assisi*)

Reflection

As we first seek to understand our spouse rather than to be understood, we move toward him/her in an act of love. When we feel understood, we feel loved.

For Discussion

1. When do you feel most understood by your spouse?
2. When do you feel least understood?
3. What will each of you do to work at better understanding your spouse?

*Roman Catholic saint.

Week 15

MARRIAGE IS A "BOAT"

Quotation

"Marriage, my dear friends, is a little boat which sails through waves and among rocks. If you lose your attention even for a moment, it will be wrecked." (Elder Aimilianos of Simonopetra)

Reflection

What an appropriate image for marriage! We must pay attention at all times as we navigate the waves and rocks we inevitably encounter in marriage so that the boat remains safe and secure.

For Discussion

1. How do you pay attention to your marriage on a regular basis?

2. What waves or rocks have you encountered in your marriage?

3. What do you do (or might you need to do) differently to pay attention to your marriage in "rough" waters so that the boat remains safe and secure?

Week 16

WHY WORRY?

Quotation

"I realized that we all worry about ourselves [and our marriages and families] too much and that only he who leaves everything to the will of God can feel truly joyous, light and peaceful." (Elder Thaddeus of Vitovnica, addition by author)

Reflection

Sometimes couples bond primarily around their worries and concerns—finances, work, children, extended family issues, etc. Imagine instead, primarily bonding with your spouse in the joy and peace of Christ—remaining responsible for the daily concerns of life but free of worry.

For Discussion

1. What are some practical steps you can each take to surrender your life to the will of God?

2. What in your marriage have you surrendered to Christ?

3. What in your marriage have you not surrendered to Christ?

4. Pay attention to and share the signs of the increased joy, peace, and lightness you experience as you surrender your lives and marriage to the will of God.

Week 17

THE MYSTERY OF MARRIAGE

Quotation

"The real mystery of marriage is not that [two people] love each other so much that they can find God in each other's lives, but that God loves them so much that they can discover each other more and more as living reminders of God's divine presence." (Henri Nouwen*)

Reflection

Imagine that at the forefront of your relationship with your spouse, you keep in mind the following truth: the love of husband and wife begins with God's unwavering love for each person, and He is the constant source and sustainer of their love for one another.

For Discussion

1. How do you see your spouse as a living reminder of God's presence?
2. How do you honor God's living presence as you relate to your spouse?
3. How can you better honor God's living presence in one another?

---

*Dutch Catholic priest, professor, writer, and theologian.

Week 18

"FILL THEIR HOUSES..."

Quotation

"Fill their houses with wheat, and wine, and oil, and with every good thing, that they may give in turn to those in need . . ."
(from The Service of Crowning in the Sacrament of Marriage)

Reflection

With so much focus on the couple in the sacrament, this petition stands out as a reminder of what is necessary to work out our salvation (Phil. 2:12) in the context of marriage. The marriage relationship is meant to support husband and wife to faithfully serve Christ together, and what couples do with material possessions reflects their life in Christ. So, it is fitting that we ask God to grant the couple everything they need materially so that they will have enough to give to "those in need" and thus heed to the words of Christ, "I was hungry and you gave me food, I was thirsty and you gave me drink, . . ." I was naked and you clothed me . . . (Matt. 25:35–36a).

For Discussion

1. How do you and your spouse practice philanthropy/ almsgiving?
2. What additional practices of giving might God be calling you to as a married couple?

Week 19

TWO ARE BETTER THAN ONE

Quotation

"Two are better than one, because they have a good reward for their toil. For if they fall, one will lift up his fellow. But woe to him who is alone when he falls and has not another to lift him up!" (Eccl. 4:9–10)

Reflection

In marriage we are not called to lean on one another as if together we make an A-Frame house, because with an A-Frame, if one side falls, both sides collapse. Rather, as the biblical writer states, if one falls, the other lifts his/her spouse. Indeed, we all fall and have moments and perhaps even periods of emotional, physical, and/or spiritual weakness when we need our spouse to lift us up.

For Discussion

1. How are each of you better as "two" than as "one"?
2. How do you lift one another up when one falls?
3. How can you do better?
4. What are some of the rewards you have received for your toil together thus far in your marriage?

Week 20

STRETCHED TO THE LIMIT?

Quotation

"If we stretch the brothers beyond measure, they will soon burst." (St. Anthony the Great)

Reflection

Though St. Anthony was speaking of monastics, married persons can also learn from the wisdom of this statement, as couples are often stretched to, or beyond their limits with the responsibilities and cares of everyday life.

For Discussion

1. What are the extraordinary ways in which your marriage is being "stretched" right now?

2. What concrete steps will you take to guard yourself and your marriage from "bursting"? Consider both preventative as well as immediate measures.

Week 21

A KEY TO NAVIGATING CONFLICT

Quotation

". . . grant me to see my own sin and not judge my brother or sister, for You are blessed to the ages of ages, Amen." (excerpt, The Prayer of Saint Ephraim)

Reflection

As married persons, we have something very significant to learn from this prayer, which is most associated with Great Lent, but significant year-round. We tend to place blame on "the other" in the face of conflict, as did Adam after he and Eve ate from the one forbidden tree in the Garden of Eden. The way of Christ, however, is to look at ourselves first.

For Discussion

1. What habit or practice will you institute to grow in awareness of your own sin and subsequently be more willing to take responsibility for your part in the face of conflict or disagreement with your spouse?

2. How can you and your spouse support one another in this discipline of growth?

Week 22

MARRIAGE AS A JOURNEY OF EXPLORATION

Quotation

"We shall not cease from exploration
And the end of all our exploring
Will be to arrive where we started
And know the place for the first time."
(T.S. Eliot*)

Reflection

This excerpt from the poem, "Little Gidding," captures beautifully the journey of marriage, the newness of Christ joining husband and wife in the sacrament of marriage, realized for the first time each day of marriage and particularly after years of a shared lifetime. If you are so inclined, read "Little Gidding" with your spouse and consider its meaning for life and its seasons.

For Discussion

1. What general connection does this poem have with marriage?
2. What do you and your spouse do consistently to "explore" the depths of one another?
3. What more can you do?
4. What surprises have you discovered about your spouse as you have come to more deeply know him/her, Christ, and yourself?

---

*American poet and playwright.

Week 23

LIVING WITH AMBIGUITY

Quotation

"Now faith is the assurance of things hoped for,
the conviction of things not seen."
(Heb. 11:1)

Reflection

We live with ambiguity every day of our lives, not knowing what might happen minute to minute, let alone day to day and so on. Nevertheless, we like to feel secure and to order our lives in such a way that we have stability.

For Discussion

1. What experience(s) of ambiguity have you experienced together?
2. What does stability look like in marriage in times of ambiguity?
3. How does faith impact your marriage, particularly in times of ambiguity?
4. How can faith more fully provide stability in your marriage in times of ambiguity?

Week 24

APPRECIATION

Quotation

"One person asked me once, 'Geronda, what is it that unites a husband and wife the most?' 'Appreciation,' I answered him." (St. Paisios)

Reflection

Appreciation is often overlooked and/or taken for granted by couples in the midst of the responsibilities of daily life. However, it is a key to genuine connection, and as we learn from St. Paisios, to unity in marriage. How simple, profound and powerful a teaching.

For Discussion

1. How do you express appreciation for your spouse (big and small ways)?

2. Consider a "discipline" of expressing appreciation to your spouse. Brainstorm about how you will put this discipline into practice daily. It need not be a big gesture.

3. After practicing this discipline for a week, discuss its impact on how you see your spouse.

Week 25

RUPTURE AND REPAIR

Quotation

"When we experience a break in connection followed by repeated attempts at repair until the bond is restored, we build implicit pathways of resilience." (Bonnie Badenoch*)

Reflection

We experience ruptures in marriage when we have a conflict we cannot resolve, a decision we cannot agree on, a
trust that has been broken, hurtful words that trigger deep
hurts, . . . When the rupture occurs, we can ignore and/
or avoid it, deepen it with harsh words or actions, or seek
to repair it. In a healthy marriage, husband and wife will
recognize when a rupture occurs and seek to repair it, perhaps not immediately if emotions are running high, but
they will come back to it for repair. The gift of repair is
that the couple will find healing for the rupture, whereas
the danger in allowing ruptures to go "un-repaired" is that
they will build and remain unhealed.

For Discussion

1. How do you navigate ruptures in your relationship?
2. What do you do well?
3. What steps can each of you take personally and
   together to improve upon how you repair ruptures
   when they occur?

---

* Marriage and family therapist and author.

Week 26

A PLACE FOR SILENCE (Part 1)

Quotation

"The tongue is our most powerful weapon of manipulation . . . If I have done some wrong thing (or even some right thing that I think you may misunderstand), I will be very tempted to help you understand my action. Silence is one of the deepest disciplines of the spirit simply because it puts the stopper on all self-justification. One of the fruits of silence is the freedom to let God be our justifier. We don't need to straighten others out." (Richard Foster*)

Reflection

We live in a world full of words, a world in which the "discipline" of silence is neither valued nor appreciated. When we are with others, silence seems awkward. We both initiate conversation and respond to what others say with words. When conflict arises, particularly in marriage or close relationships, we are often quick to want to make our point or justify our position or action.

For Discussion

1. What do you think of the value of silence as a discipline?
2. What appropriate place might silence have in your marriage?
3. How can you practice silence when you are tempted to justify yourself to your spouse?
4. How can you support one another in the practice of silence?

---

* Christian author (Quaker), theologian, whose writings focus on spiritual disciplines.

A PLACE FOR SILENCE (Part 2)

Quotation

"The beginning of freedom from anger is silence of the lips when the heart is agitated." (St. John Climacus)

Reflection

Continuing with the theme of silence, St. John gives us a directive for the discipline of silence in a very specific situation—"when the heart is agitated." That is, if either husband or wife begins to feel his/her internal temperature rise, signaling anger toward the other, it is best to be silent, and thus, not give rise to anger. What a powerful tool God gives us to stop the cycle of angry conversations with our spouse, just through the practice of silence!

For Discussion

1. Consider a signal you and your spouse can share in intense moments as a reminder for silence to restore calm before continuing a conversation in an area of disagreement.

2. What do you see as the difference between silence as a discipline and "the silent treatment"? Discuss some safeguards you will put in place so that any silence you practice in your marriage is a matter of discipline.

HARMONY
(Part 1)

Quotation

"... that He may bless them in harmony ..."
(from the Betrothal Service)

Reflection

When we think of harmony, music often comes to mind—
the blending of different tones to make a beautiful sound.
It is similar with marriage; husband and wife are two different persons who come together by God's grace to be
joined in harmony.

For Discussion

1. Discuss your personality differences (extroverted or
   introverted, structured or spontaneous, etc.)
2. How do you complement one another and create
   harmony from your differences?
3. Discuss some instances when you have experienced
   the blessing of harmony in your marriage.

Week 29

HARMONY
(Part 2)

Quotation

"... that He may bless them in harmony ..."
(from the Betrothal Service)

Reflection

Often opposites attract, and early in the relationship husband and wife rejoice in their differences and find them to be complementary. However, over time, some differences between husband and wife become sources of tension, creating disharmony in the marriage.

For Discussion

1. Discuss one personality difference that contributes to disharmony in your marriage.
2. What steps can you take to move toward harmony in areas where you have some discord with one another?

Week 30

MEANINGFUL CONVERSATION

Quotation

"If a married couple with children has fifteen minutes of uninterrupted, non-logistical, non-problem solving talk every day, I would put them in the top 5% of all married couples. It's an extraordinary achievement."
(William Doherty*)

Reflection

In our daily rhythm of married life, our conversations often center around the exchange of information—what needs to get done around the house, the children's activities, money, what happened at work, etc. We can lose sight of the heart of our spouse and begin to live parallel lives with points of contact, but even those points of contact cease to be meaningful exchanges.

Discussion

For the next week, devote daily time for meaningful conversation with one another using the following questions:

1. What was most life-giving for you today?
2. What drained the life out of you today?

---

* Professor, author, and marriage specialist.

Week 31

EVERY DAY A FEAST DAY

Quotation

"In marriage the festive joy of the first day should last for the whole life; every day should be a feast day; every day husband and wife should appear to each other as new, extraordinary beings. The only way of achieving this: let both deepen their spiritual life and strive hard in the task of self-development." (Fr. Alexander Elchaninov)

Reflection

As we mature spiritually and emotionally, Christ trans-
forms us inwardly, and thus, each day we become "new,
extraordinary beings."

For Discussion

1. What are each of you doing to deepen your spiritual
   life?
2. What are each of you doing to mature emotionally
   and intellectually?
3. What growth have you witnessed in your spouse,
   generally and specifically?

Week 32

MARRIAGE IS MORE THAN HUMAN

Quotation

"It [marriage] is a micro-kingdom, a miniature kingdom, which is the little house of the Lord." (St. Clement of Alexandria)

Reflection

When husband and wife are crowned in the sacrament of marriage, they become king and queen of a new household, the domestic church, with Christ in their midst.

For Discussion

1. How does your marriage look like a "little house of the Lord"?
2. What can you do to build upon this house of the Lord?
3. What do you need to shed so that this house better resembles a "house of the Lord"?

Week 33

PLEASANT WORDS

Quotation

"Pleasant words are like a honeycomb, sweetness to the soul and health to the body."
(Prov. 16:24)

Reflection

Sometimes in the midst of daily life and responsibilities, we forget to speak kind and pleasant words to our spouse, even if we don't typically speak harsh words. So, on one hand we may not be committing a sin of commission by speaking harsh words, but we do commit a sin of omission by being negligent in speaking pleasant words. For some, pleasant words, or words of affirmation, are the primary way in which we know we are loved. And, for all, pleasant words spoken sincerely and lovingly are "sweetness to the soul and health to the body."

For Discussion

1. What pleasant words do/would you like to hear from your spouse?

2. What pleasant words have you spoken to your spouse today, words that are "sweetness to the soul and health to the body"?

3. Take a moment to speak some sweet words to each other now and commit to speak "pleasant words" to your spouse throughout the coming week.

Week 34

RIGHT OR WRONG?

Quotation

"Even if you are right, you can be wrong."
(St. Porphyrios)

Reflection

We often have the choice to be either loving or right. For instance, in more benign situations, we may recall the details of shared memories differently. Is it worth arguing over something trivial to prove we are right? Or can we let it go, or say something like, "I remember the situation differently . . ." In more serious situations involving wrongdoing, the offended spouse may recall the situation with more severity than the offending spouse. Consciously choosing to "speak the truth in love" (Eph. 4:15) about the offense can dissipate the potential for a serious argument, yet still appropriately communicate the wrongdoing. The next time you think you are right, and your spouse is wrong about something (either facts or opinions), consider what is more important in the situation—to be right or loving?

For Discussion

1. Consider and discuss your respective tendency with one another—if you are more prone to being "right" or "loving." Consider some recent specific situations when you were faced with the choice to be "right" or "loving."

2. If your tendency is to be "right," in the coming week, commit to a "pause" when you are tempted to correct your spouse about something. Ask yourself "What is the most loving response?"

3. If your tendency is to be "loving" to the point of avoiding disagreements just to keep the peace, commit to a "pause" when you are convicted that your spouse may be wrong about something. Ask yourself, "What is really most loving in this situation? To address this or not?"

Week 35

DISCIPLINE AND SELF-DENIAL

Quotation

"Christian marriage is marked by discipline and
self-denial. Christ is the Lord even of marriage."
(Dietrich Bonhoeffer*)

Reflection

Few couples approach the sacrament of marriage with the idea that their marriage will be marked by "discipline and self-denial." Rather, they think in terms of love, warmth, companionship, partnership . . . However, spouses soon realize that authentic love in Christ involves discipline and self-denial.

For Discussion

1. How would you complete the sentence, "Christian marriage is marked by . . ."?
2. How do you exercise discipline in your marriage?
3. How do you practice self-denial in your marriage for the sake of the other?

---

*German Lutheran pastor, theologian, author, anti-Nazi dissident hanged by the Nazis.

Week 36

CULTIVATING LOVE

Quotation

"They should cultivate, as far as possible, the
virtue of love, so the two of them will always
remain united in such a way that the Third
Person—our sweetest Lord Jesus Christ—will also
remain with them." (Advice of St. Paisios for a
newly married couple)

Reflection

This wise instruction of St. Paisios reminds couples that whenever two or more are gathered in His name He is in their midst (Matt. 18:20), both within each spouse and amongst husband and wife. The more husband and wife cultivate love, that is, allow Christ to transform their imperfect love into His perfect love, His presence in their midst will grow.

For Discussion

1. What does it mean to you to cultivate love as husband and wife?
2. What practices can you put into place to be intentional about cultivating love in your marriage?
3. How do you experience the presence of "our sweetest Lord Jesus Christ" in your marriage?

Week 37

LOVE AND HARMONY

Quotation

"The love of husband and wife is the force that welds society today . . . when harmony prevails, the children are raised well, the household is kept in order . . . Great benefits, both for families and states, are thus produced." (St. John Chrysostom)

Reflection

These wise words of St. John Chrysostom are as timely today as they were in the fourth century. St. John begins with the primacy of love in marriage, a love characterized by harmony, which produces "great benefits" for families and states. Love and harmony begin with every married couple. In fact, if we take these words seriously, each married couple holds responsibility for all of society.

For Discussion

1. How is love consistently expressed and manifested in your marriage?

2. How do you nurture harmony in your marriage? Consider and discuss what more you can do to cultivate harmony.

3. How does the love and harmony in your marriage positively impact your immediate and extended family and your community?

Week 38

THE DIVINE IN THE ORDINARY

Quotation

"Marriage is a means of grace and an invitation to martyrdom, in which husband and wife learn to love and be loved by Christ in and through one another, finding the divine through the ordinary." (Fr. Stephen Muse)

Reflection

All couples have highs and lows, but mostly they live in "the ordinary," that is, the regular daily rhythm of life, somewhere in between the highs and the lows. It is precisely in the daily rhythms where we experience the love of Christ "in and through one another" as our eyes and hearts are open to receiving His grace and responding to Him.

For Discussion

1. What about marriage is a "means of grace"?
2. How have you experienced the love of Christ through your spouse in the last week?
3. How have you responded to the invitation to martyrdom in your marriage, dying to yourself, your will, for your spouse's sake?

Week 39

REPENT

Quotation

"Repent for the Kingdom of God is at hand."
(Matt. 4:17)

Reflection

What do these words of our Lord have to do with marriage? The answer is: everything! In the everyday routine of married life, we tend to fall into some bad habits with our spouse: negative communication, impatience, lack of affection, taking each other for granted, indifference, etc.—things for which we need to repent, have a change of heart/mind/focus.

For Discussion

1. Share with your spouse one bad habit you have, which disconnects you from your spouse and necessitates repentance.

2. What will you do to repent of this bad habit?

3. How can your spouse support you?

Week 40

PERFECTION?

Quotation

"There are no perfect parents, no perfect children, and there are no perfect marriages. We expect from our spouse the kind of perfection that belongs only to God."
(Fr. Anthony Coniaris)

Reflection

Sometimes we have unrealistic expectations of our spouse and of marriage—that our spouse will fulfill our every need and that we will have a storybook marriage, happily ever after. However, our spouse will not live up to expectations we may have, and marriages have struggles. Only Christ is and will remain forever perfect.

For Discussion

1. What realistic expectations do you have of your spouse?

2. What realistic expectations do you have for your marriage?

3. What expectations do you have of your spouse that only Christ can fulfill?

Week 41

CONFRONTING SIN AND WEAKNESS

Quotation

"Moses was once asked to attend an assembly
at the monastery where he resided to judge the
transgression of another brother; he refused.
When pressed, he took a basket with a hole in it,
filled it with sand, and carried it on his shoulder.
When the brothers saw him, they asked about the
basket, and he replied, "My sins run out behind
me, and I do not see them, and I am come this day
to judge failings which are not mine?" (A well-
known story about St. Moses the Black)

Reflection

When we have a conflict in marriage, we may be tempted to quickly point to a weakness in our spouse and even judge him/her, rather than to look at our weakness, which contributes to the issue at hand. This lesson from St. Moses the Black echoes our Lord's teaching, "Judge not that you be not judged. For with the judgment you pronounce you will be judged, and the measure you give will be the measure you get. Why do you see the speck that is in your brother's eye, but do not notice the log that is in your own eye? (Matt. 7:1–3).

For Discussion

1. Share with one another the last time you pointed the finger at your spouse before taking responsibility for your own shortcoming(s) in a marriage conflict.

2. Share with one another the last time you both took responsibility for your own shortcoming(s) in a conflict.

3. Determine some steps you will take together to grow in taking responsibility for your own weaknesses.

Week 42

EMOTIONAL INTELLIGENCE

Quotation

"Happily married couples . . . have hit upon a dynamic that keeps their negative thoughts and feelings about each other (which all couples have) from overwhelming their positive ones . . . they have . . . an emotionally intelligent marriage." (John Gottman* and Nan Silver**)

Reflection

Some of us are more prone to negative thinking about ourselves and those around us. Others are more prone to seeing the good, sometimes to a fault. Our general tendency is reflected in how we think about and feel toward our spouse. Part of exercising discipline in marriage is to not succumb to the passion of entertaining negative thoughts and feelings toward our spouse.

For Discussion

1. Discuss each of your tendencies in regard to thoughts and feelings.

2. When was the last time you entertained a positive thought and/or feeling toward your spouse?

3. When was the last time you entertained a negative thought and/or feeling toward your spouse?

4. For the next week, take five minutes daily to express to each other something you appreciate about your spouse from your interactions that day.

---

* American psychologist and author, specializing in marriage research and therapy.
** Author, journalist and editor.

Week 43

DRAWING NEAR TO GOD

Quotation

"Marriage is the key to moderation and the harmony of desires, the seal of a deep friendship . . . the unique drink from a fountain enclosed, inaccessible to those without. For marriage does not remove God, but brings all closer to Him, for it is God Himself who draws us to it." (St. Gregory the Theologian)

Reflection

These words of St. Gregory offer a beautiful mosaic of the nature of Christian marriage. Read this passage out loud twice, one to the other, slowly and deliberately. Close your eyes when you are listening and just soak in the words.

For Discussion

1. What does "harmony of desires" mean to you?
2. What does your friendship look like, and how do you nourish it?
3. What in your marriage is private and inaccessible "to those without"?
4. How has marriage drawn you closer to God?

---

*Given the scope of this passage, you may want to meet twice to discuss it.

Week 44

WORDS OF CONSOLATION

Quotation

". . . you who are married, when you approach your spouse; . . . Whatever you say, whatever you think of saying, say it only after you've said a word or two which will give others joy, consolation, a breath of life." (Elder Aimilianos of Simonopetra)

Reflection

What beautiful words of counsel for all our relationships, beginning with our marriage! What a gift we would offer to our spouse if we began all our conversations with words that "give joy, consolation, a breath of life" particularly before beginning a difficult conversation.

For Discussion

1. How do you tend to begin conversations with your spouse?
2. What words do you typically speak to your spouse that give "joy, consolation, a breath of life"?
3. What words of "joy, . . ." would you like to hear more from your spouse?

In the next week, be intentional about using words your spouse desires to hear from you.

Week 45

FINANCES

Quotation

"For where your treasure is, there your heart will be also." (Matt. 6:21)

Reflection

Research shows that money is a source of conflict for many couples, often involving matters of spending habits. However, we need to dig a bit deeper to determine the underlying value we place on money. Status? Security? Enjoyment? Control? Something else? Christ teaches us something radical here. Money is a matter of faith; how we view money and what we do with it is at the heart of our Christian faith.

For Discussion

1. What is the primary value you place on money? Is it the same or different for each of you? If different, how do you navigate the difference so that it does not become an issue?

2. Consider together one way in which you can grow in faithfulness to Christ with the "treasure" you have been given. Then determine how you will follow through.

Week 46

LISTENING AS HOSPITALITY

Quotation

"True listeners no longer have an inner need to make their presence known. They are free to receive, to welcome, to accept. Listening is much more than allowing another to talk while waiting for a chance to respond. Listening is paying full attention to others [our spouse] and welcoming them [him/her] into our very beings. The beauty of listening is that those who are listened to start feeling accepted, start taking their words more seriously and discovering their own true selves. Listening is a form of spiritual hospitality by which you invite strangers [your spouse] to become friends, to get to know their inner selves more fully, and even to dare to be silent with you." (Henri Nouwen*, additions by author)

Reflection

Have you ever thought of listening as a form of hospitality, an opportunity to exercise freedom, a means of accepting your spouse? In the frantic lives we often lead, do we take the time to pause and truly listen to our spouse? A very common complaint among couples is that they do not feel understood by their spouse. Perhaps if we offered spiritual hospitality to our spouse in the form of listening, that complaint would be remedied.

For Discussion

1. What do you think of the concept of listening as "spiritual hospitality"?
2. How do you listen well to your spouse?
3. What can you do differently/better in listening to your spouse?
4. Take turns sharing something with your spouse. To the person on the listening end: simply receive then reflect to your spouse what you have heard, using your own words.

---

*Dutch Catholic priest, professor, writer, and theologian.

Week 47

COMMITMENT AND TRUST

Quotation

"Commitment to and trust in one's spouse are foundational to a good marriage." (Anonymous)

Reflection

Marriage experts agree on the importance of commitment and trust for the marriage relationship to survive, grow, and thrive.

For Discussion

1. How does your life in Christ both inform and impact your commitment to and trust in your spouse?
2. Complete the following sentence for each other: "I most trust you to . . ."
3. Then complete this sentence for each other: "I need to grow to trust you more to . . ."
4. What is one thing you can each do to contribute to the growth of commitment and trust for one another?

THE OVERARCHING LITMUS TEST

Quotation

"Let all that you do be done in love."
(1 Cor. 16:14)

Reflection

St. Paul's admonition to the people in Corinth and to us is unequivocal. The litmus test for all we do is love. The question to ask ourselves in all situations with everyone: what is the most loving thing to do? Unfortunately, in the moment, we do not always pause to ask that question, and we may speak or act without even thinking, especially with those closest to us, including our spouse. Acting in love is a choice we make.

For Discussion

1. When is it easiest for you to speak or act in love toward your spouse?

2. When do you find it more difficult to speak or act in love toward your spouse?

3. What steps can you take to encourage each other to pause and ask this question when you are tempted to respond to your spouse from a place other than love?

Week 49

RITUALS

Quotation

". . . rituals play very important functions in human societies. They help individuals through their anxieties, connect to one another. They help people find meaning in their lives." (Dimitris Xygalatas*)

Reflection

As Orthodox Christians we know the importance of ritual—making the sign of the cross, a daily "rule" of prayer, preparing for and receiving the Eucharist. . . . Research in the social sciences also acknowledges the importance of rituals in our daily lives. In fact, one study found that embracing or kissing one's spouse at the beginning and end of each day was the one ritual that made a consistent difference in maintaining a stable, happy marriage.

For Discussion

1. What rituals do you and your spouse have that nurture love and connection? (Hint: we have a lot more rituals in our lives than we often realize!)

2. What new rituals might you consider to further grow connection with your spouse?

---

*Cognitive anthropologist and professor whose research focuses on the study of ritual behaviors.

Week 50

THE EXPERIENCE OF LOVE

Quotation

"A single, vivid experience of love will advance us much farther, will far more surely protect our souls from evil, than the most arduous struggle against sin." (Alexander Elchaninov)

Reflection

If our eyes and hearts are open, we will recognize our encounters with love—the love of God in Jesus Christ manifested in and through many experiences in life—worship, prayer, reading Scripture or other devotional books, the beauty of God's creation in nature, God's love manifested through others, etc. For those who are married, God's love is experienced in and through our spouse, in both big and small ways. While we may feel compelled to share a wrong or negative point with our spouse, it is not always necessary to do so. However, creating opportunities to share a powerful expression of love is always necessary and loving!

For Discussion

1. What would you consider to be a "vivid experience of love" from your spouse?

2. Recall and share with one another a "vivid experience of love" in your marriage.

3. How did it impact you?

WHAT DO WE SEE?

Quotation

"Unless we look at a person and see the beauty
there is in this person, we can contribute
nothing to him. One does not help a person by
discerning what is wrong, what is ugly, what is
distorted. Christ looked at everyone he met, at the
prostitute, at the thief, and saw the beauty hidden
there. Perhaps it was distorted, perhaps damaged,
but it was beauty none the less, and what he
did was to call out this beauty." (Metropolitan
Anthony Bloom)

Reflection

In the rush of daily life, we may not pause, prioritize and take the time to look at and truly see the beauty in our spouse, both on the inside and outside. However, if we have a bone to pick, we are quick to point the finger.

For Discussion

1. What are three points of outward beauty you see in your spouse right now?
2. What are three points of inward beauty you most appreciate about your spouse?
3. For the next week, attentively look at your spouse to "see" him/her, and once daily "call out" his/her beauty.

Week 52

WISDOM FOR CONFLICT

Quotation

"The one who first states a case seems right, until the other comes and cross-examines."
(Prov. 18:17)

Reflection

Sometimes conflict in marriage arises from husband and wife recalling details of an event or situation differently. When this happens, remember that we all see things through our own filters. When we listen attentively to our spouse and seek to understand his/her perspective, rather than cross-examine him/her, we open the door to the opportunity to grow toward one another.

For Discussion

1. What is your tendency when conflict arises in your marriage—to get caught up in factual details or to see the bigger picture?

2. In conflict, do you listen attentively and offer grace or cross-examine?

3. Recall a recent conflict and how you treated one another in the midst of it.

Bonus 1

OBEDIENCE

Quotation

"Husband and wife are to be subject to one another out of reverence for Christ (Eph. 5:21). No marriage can work if the two do not sacrifice their own wills in loving obedience." (Archimandrite Vassilios Papavassiliou)

Reflection

Mutual submission/obedience is a hallmark of a healthy, whole marriage. Each day husband and wife sacrifice their own wills for the sake of the other. After all is not self-sacrifice a hallmark of the love of God in Jesus Christ, the same love we are called to extend to all, beginning with our closest neighbor, our spouse?

For Discussion

1. How do you sacrifice your own will in obedience to your spouse? Be specific with ways in which you are obedient to your spouse and ways in which you experience your spouse being obedient to you.

2. What is difficult for you to sacrifice for your spouse?

Bonus 2

"THE" RULE OF MARRIAGE

Quotation

"God gave you Christ as the foundation of your marriage. 'Welcome one another, therefore, as Christ has welcomed you, for the glory of God' (Rom. 15:7). In a word, live together in the forgiveness of your sins, for without it no human fellowship, least of all a marriage, can survive. Don't insist on your rights, don't blame each other, don't judge or condemn each other, don't [find] fault with each other, but accept each other every day from the bottom of your hearts. . . . From the first day of your wedding till the last, the rule must be: 'Welcome one another . . . for the glory of God.'" (Dietrich Bonhoeffer*, from a sermon he wrote from prison for his niece's wedding)

Reflection

Consider and ponder welcoming your spouse as Christ welcomes you to be foundational for your marriage. In other words, making your marriage a sacred space of hospitality/welcoming. In this excerpt, Bonhoeffer not only articulates the general "rule" for marriage, but also what it means day to day.

For Discussion

1. In Bonhoeffer's description of the day-to-day practices of welcoming one another, what most resonates with you?
2. Which practices do you do well as a couple?
3. Which of the practices is a growth point for you?
4. How will you deliberately work on making the growth point a strength?

---

*German Lutheran pastor, theologian, author, anti-Nazi dissident hanged by the Nazis.

Bonus 3

LISTENING

Quotation

"Listening is love delivered." (Dr. Albert Rossi)

Reflection

When our spouse communicates something to us about a difficult topic or a source of conflict, our tendency is to listen with an ear toward responding. We would do well to "deliver" love to our spouse by listening to hear and understand what he/she is saying, beginning with repeating back to our spouse in our own words what we have heard him/her say.

For Discussion

1. What do you think of listening as "love delivered"?
2. How do you listen well to your spouse? How does your spouse listen well to you?
3. What can each of you do to more attentively listen to one another?

Bonus 4

FIDELITY

Quotation

"What marriage offers—and what fidelity is meant to protect—is the possibility of moments when what we have chosen and what we desire are the same. Such a convergence obviously cannot be continuous. No relationship can continue very long at its highest emotional pitch. But fidelity prepares us for the return of these moments, which give us the highest joy we can know; that of union, communion . . ." (Wendell Berry*)

Reflection

Fidelity in marriage means faithfulness at all times and in all circumstances, which according to Berry, allows for the possibility of those moments where we experience with our spouse a deep sense of union and communion, that is, "oneness."

For Discussion

1. What are some of the concrete ways in which you are faithful to one another as husband and wife?
2. Share with one another one "moment" of "highest joy" in your marriage, when you felt a deep sense of communion with your spouse.

---

*Renowned American writer, farmer, and activist whose Christian faith informs his connection to God's creation and the environment.

Bonus 5

UNITY

Quotation

"Unity doesn't always mean agreement."
(Dn. Michael Hyatt)

Reflection

Sometimes we think we need to agree on everything to have unity in our marriage, and the small things we disagree on become bigger than they really are. Being aligned with our spouse on the important matters of marriage is key; if we know we are on the same path in marriage, if we agree on the purpose of marriage, then disagreements along the way will not seem so looming. That is, when couples are secure in the "big things" then other disagreements take their proper place as "little things."

For Discussion

1. What do you understand to be the primary goals/purposes of marriage?
2. What is the pathway to realize these goals?
3. Take note of any differences in the big things and consider discussing further with your priest.

EMOTIONAL CAPITAL

Quotation

"Marriages become troubled essentially by wasting the emotional capital in negative emotions . . ." (Fr. Stephen Muse)

Reflection

When husband and wife choose gratitude and emotional investment in what they love and appreciate in their spouse, they draw nearer to one another. When they focus on and entertain negative emotions toward the other, they distance themselves from one another.

For Discussion

1. Which positive emotions do you regularly have for your spouse?

2. Which negative emotions do you tend to engage toward your spouse?

3. How will you divest the negative emotions and invest in the positive emotions in the next week?

Acknowledgments

This workbook represents selected entries from the "Becoming One" posts of the Center for Family Care of the Greek Orthodox Archdiocese of America. Many thanks to my co-workers, Fr. Alexander Goussetis, Prevytera Melanie DiStefano, and Mari McMullen for their continual encouragement and input over the last several years. For each entry, all my co-workers have contributed feedback, editing, and design. A special thanks to Presvytera Eleni Christakos who graciously sorted through and formatted the entries. Thanks to my husband, best friend and partner of forty-three years with whom I am growing daily toward oneness. Finally, and most importantly, thank you Lord Jesus Christ, for your abiding and faithful presence in marriage. In the words of Elder Aimilianos of Blessed Memory: "In marriage, . . . the man marries the woman, and the woman marries the man, but the two together also marry Christ. So, three take part in the mystery, and the three remain together for life."

Quotation Sources

Week:

1. Matt. 22:37-39
2. Henri Nouwen, *Out of Solitude*
3. C. S. Lewis, *Mere Christianity*
4. John Gottman, *Why Marriages Succeed or Fail*
5. Gen. 3:12-13
6. 1 Cor. 13:4-7
7. 1 Cor. 13:4
8. 1 Cor. 13:4
9. 1 Cor. 13:4b–5a

10. St. Paisios, *Spiritual Counsels, Volume IV, Family Life*

11. Anonymous

12. St. Mark the Ascetic, "St. Mark on Those Who Think They are Made Right by Works: Two Hundred and Twenty-Six Texts," *The Philokalia: The Complete Text (Vol. 1)*

13. John Gottman and Nan Silver, *The Seven Principles for Making Marriage Work*

14. The Prayer of St. Francis of Assisi

15. Elder Aimilianos, «Marriage: The Great Sacrament,» in *The Church at Prayer,* by Archimandrite Aimilianos of Simonopetra

16. Elder Thaddeus of Vitovnica, *Our Thoughts Determine Our Lives*

17. Henri Nouwen, *Clowning in Rome: Reflections on Solitude, Celibacy, Prayer, and Contemplation*

18. The Service of Crowning in the Sacrament of Marriage

19. Eccl. 4:9–10

20. St. Anthony the Great, *Sayings of the Desert Fathers,* by Benedicta Ward

21. The Prayer of Saint Ephraim

22. T.S. Eliot, "Little Gidding"

23. Heb. 11:1

24. St. Paisios, *Spiritual Counsels, Volume IV, Family Life*

25. Bonnie Badenoch, *The Heart of Trauma: Healing the Embodied Brain in the Context of Relationships*

26. Richard Foster

27. St. John Climacus, *Ladder of Divine Ascent*

28. The Betrothal Service

29. The Betrothal Service
30. William Doherty, *The Intentional Family*
31. Fr. Alexander Elchaninov, *The Diary of a Russian Priest*
32. St. Clement of Alexandria
33. Prov. 16:24
34. St. Porphyrios, *Wounded by Love*
35. Dietrich Bonhoeffer, *The Cost of Discipleship* (trans. K. V. Munchen)
36. St. Paisios, *Spiritual Counsels 4: Family Life*
37. St. John Chrysostom, *On Marriage and Family Life*
38. Fr. Stephen Muse, "Marriage Encounter at the Altar of the Heart," interview with Fr. Alexander Goussetis, Family Matters Podcast, Ancient Faith
39. Matt. 4:17
40. Fr. Anthony Coniaris, from a personal conversation
41. Story from life of St. Moses the Black, www.mosestheblack.org
42. John Gottman and Nan Silver, *The Seven Principles for Making Marriage Work*
43. St. Gregory the Theologian, "Poem in Praise of Virginity," in *On God and Man: The Theological Poetry of St. Gregory of Nazianzus*
44. Elder Aimilianos, "Marriage: The Great Sacrament," in *The Church at Prayer,* by Archimandrite Aimilianos of Simonopetra
45. Matt. 6:21
46. Henri Nouwen, *Bread for the Journey*
47. Anonymous
48. 1 Cor. 16:14

49. Dimitris Xygalatas, *Ritual: How Seemingly Senseless Acts Make Life Worth Living*

50. Fr. Alexander Elchaninov, *The Diary of a Russian Priest*

51. Metropolitan Anthony Bloom, *Beauty and Meaning: The T. S. Eliot Lectures of the Most Reverend Anthony Bloom*

52. Prov. 18:17

Bonus Entries:

1. Archimandrite Vassilios Papavassiliou, *Thirty Steps to Heaven: The Ladder of Divine Ascent for All Walks of Life*

2. Deitrich Bonhoeffer, a wedding sermon written from prison for his niece, www.fiercemarriage.com/a-wedding-sermon-from-a-1943-prison-cell-dietrich-bonhoeffer

3. Dr. Albert Rossi, *Becoming a Healing Presence*

4. Wendell Berry, *The Art of the Commonplace: The Agrarian Essays*

5. Dn. Michael Hyatt, from Keynote address, "God's Threefold Purpose in Marriage," at Pastoral Challenges in Marriage Conference hosted by the Center for Family Care, Greek Orthodox Archdiocese of America, 2020 (entire keynote can be found at: www.youtube.com/watch?v=PLhupQ_06pQ

6. Fr. Stephen Muse, "Marriage Encounter at the Altar of the Heart," interview with Fr. Alexander Goussetis, Family Matters Podcast, Ancient Faith

www.ingramcontent.com/pod-product-compliance
Lightning Source LLC
LaVergne TN
LVHW051744080426
835511LV00018B/3223